Let Me Be Libra

NNEKA

Order this book online at **www.trafford.com**
or email orders@trafford.com

Most Trafford titles are also available at major online book retailers.

Works have appeared in several antholgies, including "Poems by Blacks, Volume 1
&11. Poem "Blues is a Woman," performed at the Musuem of African American Art
in Tampa Florida. She done several readings in her Philadelphia, her hometown.

Printed in the United States of America.

ISBN: 978-1-4669-0720-1 (sc)
ISBN: 978-1-4669-0722-5 (hc)
ISBN: 978-1-4669-0721-8 (e)

Library of Congress Control Number: 2011962413

Trafford rev. 12/15/2011

 www.trafford.com

North America & International
toll-free: 1 888 232 4444 (USA & Canada)
phone: 250 383 6864 ♦ fax: 812 355 4082

To Leon, Christian, Chavonne, Quentin, Demetrius, Ciara, Ryan, and Aaron

For the love and sunshine you bring into my life each day.

Love always, Nana

Introduction

Writing was like a soothing balm or quiet friend-comforting. I discovered solitude in writing (and reading poetry). For me, writing poetry gave life to the words I often found difficult to say out loud. It was as if writing gave life to my unspoken voice. It was my own personal journey that gave meaning and order to my life.

There are some special people I want to thank for helping me on my writing journey. First, I want to thank you, my beautiful daughters; Leslie, Desiree, Deirdre and Charisse, for your inspiration. Next, thank you my generous son, Richard, for your encouragement.

I thank Naeema for quiet times. Thank you, Bobbi for butterflies. I thank Justine, for the fun times.

A special thanks to George, for believing and always being there for me.

Patricia (Nneka) Ford

Contents

Dedications

Reflections

Part One: On living, loving, and dreaming.

These poems express my feelings;
and the need to find some order in my life.

Part Two: Dedications.

These poems are dedicated to those people that stirred
my imagination with their creativity.

Reflections:

These are some left-over thoughts that had no place to go.
They are not poems, merely fragmented thoughts.

Let me be the space

That flows through your life
Let me be the sweet taste
In your mouth
Let me share the peace
You wish for
Let me touch that
Secret place in your
Life
Let me be the key that
Unlock the hidden door
Of your soul
Let me
    Let me
        Let me

A hand full of dreams

A hand full of dreams
A pocket full of love
A room full of laughter

The memories are vivid
The thoughts are few
My needs are so simple
A hand full of dreams
A lifetime with you

Blues is a Woman

Blues is a woman . . . in her cryin' time
Blues is a woman . . . with rough raw edges
Yet easy and mellow
Like a Coltrane tune
Blues is a woman . . . singin' and cryin'
And damn near dying
Yet soft and sweet
Like a Miles tune
(and we all know how
he can get)
Blues is a woman alright
mean and hard . . .
Mad as all hell
yet tender and smooth
Like when Lady sings
when she be feelin' good
Blues is a sweet thing
     A bitter thing
Blues is a woman

Winter people—summer people

Winter people are cold
with cold frowning faces
Is it the weather?

Summer people are warm
With warm smiling faces
Is it the weather?

Some people are winter
people in the summertime
Some people are summer
people in the wintertime

few people are summer people
all the time

Black Song

I am a song-a black song
A loud wild untamed song
I fly on the wings of the wind
My voice screaming at the sky
I am as dark and mysterious
As the night
Created out of the heart
Of my people
Nourished by their tears
Like a flower is nourished
By the rain
I grew strong proud and fearless
I am a song-a black song

Home

A blind man on the corner
    Singin the blues
        Off key
But then maybe he is not
        Off key
Maybe it's those folks listenin is
        Off key
He told me once
Chile I can see round the corner
    Clear into the future
Like I knew my baby was goin
    To leave me when she
Brought home that red dress
An had the nerve to lie to me
Tellin me the damn dress was green
Even dumb blind folks know
Red feel hot and green feel cool
She should have known better than
To lie to me cause I can see round
The corner right into the future
But I just laughed and told her

Honey that green dress sure
Look good on yo brown body
But chile I bet her bed is
Colder than mine now
Cause I can see round the corner
Clear into the future

Let me be Libra

Let me be patient
Let me love
Let my beauty shine

Let me show mercy
Let me create
Let me open doors

Let me dance
Let me give peace
Let me find order

Let me be Libra

Clouds and dreams

Clouds and dreams
        Always there
Just out of reach
        Hovering overhead
        Clouds are real
        Dreams are real
Clouds fill the empty
        Void in the sky
Dreams fill the empty
        Void in the heart
        Search the clouds
        Search the dreams
Find the peace hidden within

Something found

I found the days are longer now
I found time is no longer my enemy
I found something special in each day
Like the sound of laughter
I found pleasure in watching butterflies
And joy and contentment in solitude
Most of all I found another part of
Me to celebrate what I found

A Piano

I am a piano
The cool keys
Blending with warm
Fingers
Making beautiful
Music
The white keys
The black keys
I was with
The composer
In his quiet place
When he composed
I am a piano
A lingering melody
An eternal lingering
Melody

On the way to self

On the way to myself I got lost
Instead of going ahead
I was going backwards
Yet it felt OK because the
Past and I were on familiar terms
The future was frightening
Well—not knowing what
Could happen
But I was on the way to my self

On the way to myself there were
All kind of spaces and places
Inside of me that laughed and
Cried and some places that were
Not touched at all
Some places were all torn apart
To make way for the new me

On the way to myself I found
New spaces new places
On the way to myself—I found
You
And the journey continues—

Essence of a Poem

A poem is like a quiet morning
A quiet lazy morning
With dew drenched flowers
And warm left over thoughts

A poem is like a lover's kiss
Soft and sweet wanting more
Holding hands
Walking on a lonely beach

A poem is like a rainy day
Or the fragrance of wet grass
Or wandering through
A magical garden of butterflies

Living inside a Poem

Let me wrap you in a poem
A poem that will caress you
A poem that will warm you
A poem as large as
Tree covered mountains
A poem as wide
As a child's smile
Let me wrap you in a poem
That will keep you
From being lonely
Wrap you in a poem
That will be yours alone
That you can keep
Or share
That you can wrap
Around someone
Then we all
Will be poets

There will always be butterflies

When harsh days of winter seems endless
And icy wind blows
When sidewalks wear a coat of ice
When days are gray and bleak
And nights are long and cold
When looking out of windows
At deserted streets
And the only sound you hear
is your own voice
And the only faces you see
Are bitter frowning faces
When there is no grass
Or summer flowers
Remember
          There will always be butterflies

Shadappy

I experience this often
Difficult to separate the two
Two dominant emotions housed in the same space
Two dominant emotions taking up the same space
Both longing to inhabit that place where there is
Only room for one
Each with an urgent need to be met
Sad because . . . . yet . . .
Happy because . . . . yet . . .
What would Freud say?
What would Jung say?
How would they distinguish it?
Is there therapy for shadappy?
Is it something I ate?
Too much sweet
Too much sour
Or was it the sweet /sour chicken
That caused me to be shadappy?

Youth of old age

For Randall Robinson
"Quitting America"

I too have" arrived safely at the
Youth of old age"
I brought along precious memories
I planted seeds of happiness
I invented my own space
With permission and blessings
From the universe
I have chosen my own time
Drinking deep from the cup
Of love
Rolling its sweet taste
Deliciously over my tongue
Welcoming butterflies in summer
Snowflakes in winter
Yes I have arrived safely
At the youth of old age
As I dance and celebrate
The new era of my soul

A rainbow of tears

Life is like a rainbow of tears
There is sadness and beauty
One can not experience one without the other
           Yet, there is the promise of
           A rainbow across the horizon
That follows the rain (tears from heaven)
Imagine, a rainbow of tears flowing
Through life
Then imagine, His touch in
The rainbow of tears

Praise to the universe

I sing a song to the universe
A song of praise
A joyful song
Lifting my voice
A song to join the song
Of birds of the morning
Our song will give a sweet
Sound to the morning
Our song
Will blend with the gentle breeze
Causing the trees to dance
This is a praise song to the universe
A song of thanksgiving
A song of hope
A joyful song

What's inside

Pieces scattered
Precious pieces—like crystals
I see a reflection of images
Captured for a brief moment
The glue that holds it all
Together . . . .
My memories

Celebration

Today I celebrate this new era of my soul
I celebrate the 'butterfly season'
I celebrate my new bones
I celebrate bright colors—purple and red
I celebrate a new identity—Nana
I celebrate as I hug trees
Yesterday my soul did not celebrate
This new era
Tomorrow I will celebrate anew

Yes, Virginia there is a God

Yes, Virginia there is a God
You see him in a field of
New fallen snow
Or while watching the clouds
Floating in the sky
You see him when
You see a rainbow
You see him on a starry night

You hear him when the wind
Rustle through the trees
You hear him when birds sing
Or the chirping of crickets
On a quiet summer night

You feel his touch when
A soft breeze
Blows against your face
Or when you feel
Someone's pain
Or share someone's joy

You see him in
The beauty of nature
You hear in the
Sound of children laughing
You touch him by
Reaching out to others
Yes, Virginia there is a God

Composition of a star

God took the gleam from
An angel's eye
He took the sparkle from
A baby's smile
He captured fire from
The noon day sun
And the purity of a dove
He fashioned the likeness of
A diamond
Deep inside the earth
He took a wish from
A mother's heart
      And He made a star

What color is love

What color is love
Is it green
The color of a tree
In full bloom
Is it blue
The color of
A cloudless sky
Or is it gold
The color
Of the first
Light of a new day
What color is love
Is it many colors
The color
Of a flowered cover meadow
What color is love
It's the color of
Happiness

Dancing in a dream

A soft song whispering in my ear
To the tune of piano playing
A melody of love
An almost forgotten melody
Wasn't love to be forever
Like summer flowers
And autumn leaves
Oh how I miss your sleepy kisses
So I wrap myself in these memories
And dance with you
In a dream

Little Brown Children

Little brown children
    Playing in the sun
    Follow the leader one by one
    Open arms and laughing faces
    Dreams of time and distant places

Little brown children
    Playing in the sand
    Reaching out for an
    Outstretched hand
    Chasing butterflies
    Picking flowers
    Making use of precious hours

To my Sisters

Work hard during the day
Cry long during the night
To my sisters
Those that comfort
Those that share
We know the pain
Of losing
We know the joy
Of loving
To my sisters
Our common bond is
Our black skin
The strong lifeline
That holds us together
Through tears
Still we be
Through laughter
Still we be
To my sisters
Of yesterday
That showed the way
To my sisters
Of today
That show courage
To my sisters
Of tomorrow
That will carry on

To Wynton 4/16/89

1

you picked up your trumpet caressing it
as man caresses a woman-with liquid fingers
your laughing eyes gazing at the golden body
glistening in the light
a melodic sound danced in your head
you gave this sound to the world
when you picked up your trumpet

11

boy what you know 'bout the blues
what you know 'bout being lonesome
cause some sugar-mouth woman left you
or you tired from working from sunup to sundown
boy you never felt pain
no boy you don't know the blues
yes sir but I've heard Billie singing
    I've heard Trane playing
and I know they were hurting sir
    I have a sound a sound in my head
that needs to come out
yes sir I know about the blues

111

a syncopated sound in muted tones
screaming to be free black codes
a familiar yet unknown rhythm black codes
reaching back for a melody as old as time
yet as new as tomorrow
blues went underground
    came out new and vibrant
        black codes

To Sonny (summer '79)

My thoughts go round in circles
Traveling in and round
The corners of my mind
Like a breeze blowing
Thru the black spaces
Where I hid my memories
(Always picking some debris)
My thoughts go round in circles
Lingering over the soft places
Round and round in circles
Always returning to you

The Parasol Lady

For Judith Jamison (2/10/89)

I saw your tall lean body
Your slender arms
Waving over the crowd
You said you were glad
To be back
We were honored to
Have you in our presence
        You danced before
        The crown heads of Europe
        Your beauty—your grace
Your laughing eyes
        They were mere mortals
        In your presence
Wade in the water
        Dance in the water
        Touch the troubled water
        Bring your troubled
        Soul to the water
Wade in the water children
The parasol lady will
Dance for you

To Gwendolyn Brooks
(The quiet poet)

She spoke softly/with velvet words
Her determined brown face
Etched with lines/memory lines
Placed there by years and tears
Her manner was as soft as her voice
Her words soft but like arrows
Shot straight to the target
She told of brownstone houses
Brown skinned girls
   Old people
   Young people
   Our people
The quiet poet
Thru the years
She raised consciousness
At time she would raise hell
She 'jazzed June'
She 'Beckons' us

She peopled a nation with
   Her people
   "Maude Martha"
   "The Bean Eaters"
   She bared her soul
   Showing us what life
   Is all about
   Sometimes ugly
   Sometimes beautiful
   The velvet tongue poet

Lady & the Blues

(For Billie, Bessie, and Dinah)

The lady sings the blues tonight
She wears the blues
       like a satin gown
       like the flower in her hair
The lady know the blues
       like the lines on her soft face
       like the taste of stale cigarettes
and warm coffee

The lady sings the blues tonight
         in a smoke filled room
         at a table for one
         looking in a cracked mirror
The lady sings the blues

Poet to poet
(for Keton)

Pt. 1

The beginning of time
Words connected across time like a chain—
Connecting heart mind feeling
Words connecting worlds
Words that heal
Words that lash out
Words as old as time
Words as new as tomorrow

Poetry is the sound
Of the universe
OM-OM-OM
The single sound
Linking the soul
To the universe since

Ancient bards tell of
A time long ago
Ancient bards with
Tongues like honey-sweet

Pt. 2

Captivating the imagination
O' ancient unknown bards
Your words your thoughts
Leaping across centuries
Tantalizing—creating images
Linking kindred souls

Dare to see the world
Through the eyes of a poet
Dare to think poet thoughts
Poet to poet

Thank you Zora

To Zora Neale Hurston
She wore her hat at a reckless angle
She approached life the same way

Zora, I thank you for allowing me—
Through your writing
To know it's alright
To be me black woman whole
You showed me it's ok to be washed
In the healing waters
To be my own butterfly
To leap first then try my wings
Through you writing
You have allowed
Our mothers our sisters
Their blackness and be loved unashamed
And dance to the tune
Of her own tears

To Myrtle

You too have arrived safely to the
Youth of old age
And have planted seeds of contentment
You have allowed your children
Permission to try their wings
And to fly unafraid
You taught them to pray, to love, to trust
That they allowed their children
Permission to try their wings
To pray, to love, to trust
Your eternal smile is the
Sunshine that guides them
With open arms you welcome
Those fortunate enough to
Be your 'forever' friends
Myrtle you are
    Mother
    Youthful
    Righteous
    Tender
    Loving
    Enduring

Psalm 139v.14
. . . I will praise thee for I am fearful and wonderfully made . . .
God bless you

(for Rod McKuen's 'Season in the Sun')
"Write me a poem"

I will write you a poem
Of sunshine and love
Of clouds and dreams
Of pain and laughter
Of time and memories

We all have a prisoner
    locked within
    the key to the door
rust—turns to ashes in our hands

Here's to the child
    locked inside
    crying to be free

(On clouds and dreams)

Clouds and dreams
    They are real
Neither can be captured
Neither can be touched
    Clouds and dreams

The sunshine years and
The midnight years of
Our lives are so far apart
Can the clouds or dreams
Bring them closer

About the author

Pat Ford (Nneka) resides in Philadelphia. Her works have appeared in several anthologies including "Poems by Blacks, Volume I & II. Her poem "Blues is a Woman" was performed at the Museum of African American Art, in Tampa, Florida. She has done several readings locally. Her poem, "Living inside a poem," was published in Philly Ink as part of Larry Robin's 100 poets' series.

Her poem "winter people/summer people" was set to music and premiered in Philadelphia.

Currently, Pat is working on a collection of short stories called "Summer People."

Pat enjoys traveling and spending time with her grandchildren and great-grandchild.

Her goal as a poet/writer is to recognize and realize the blessing from the universe. But most importantly, to connect with others writers for sharing, growing and healing.

Printed in the United States
By Bookmasters